guide to the national museum

vincent van gogh

amsterdam

Edition: © b.v. 't Lanthuys, Amsterdam

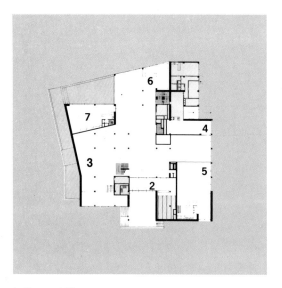

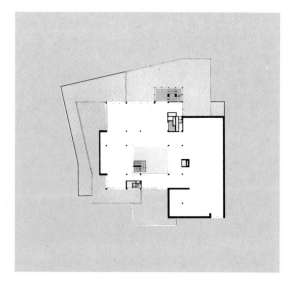

1. Ground Floor
   2 entrance
   3 exhibition
   4 library
   5 arts workshop
   6 reproduction department
   7 restaurant

2. Exhibition

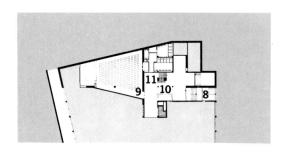

0. Basement
   8 service entrance
   9 Theo van Gogh room
   10 exhibition
   11 toilets

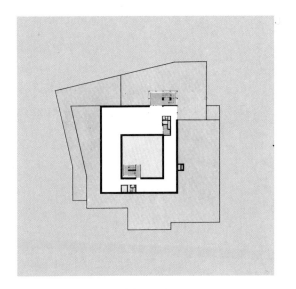

3. Drawings and graphic works

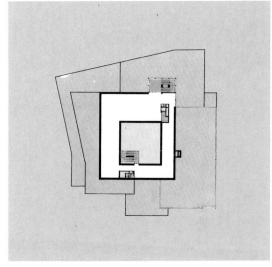

4. Exhibition

Dr V.W. van Gogh (1890–1978), son of Theo and Jo

The Potato Eaters / Nuenen, April 1885   oil / canvas, 82 × 114 cm

The National Museum Vincent van Gogh was built as a permanent home for a collection of paintings, drawings, graphic art and documents by Vincent Willem van Gogh (1853–1890), and works by his friends and contemporaries, who included Gauguin and Toulouse-Lautrec. The collection belonged to Vincent's younger brother, Theodorus van Gogh (1857–1891), and after his death it was administered with love and dedication by his widow, Johanna Gesina van Gogh-Bonger (1862–1925). On her death this task passed to their son, Dr V.W. van Gogh (1890–1978), who was named after the artist.

In 1931 the Van Gogh family came to an agreement with the City of Amsterdam whereby the collection was placed on permanent display in the Stedelijk Museum. Apart from the war years, Vincent's paintings remained in the Stedelijk until the opening of the Van Gogh Museum in 1973.

On 21 July 1962 the Dutch state signed an agreement with the Vincent van Gogh Foundation (founded 1960) providing for the establishment of the National Vincent van Gogh Museum. This was done in order to prevent the collection from being dispersed on the death of Dr Van Gogh, and in the interests of continued public access.

The following parties contributed to the agreement:

The Van Gogh family, which announced that it was prepared to transfer its holdings of paintings, drawings and documents to the Vincent van Gogh Foundation.

The Vincent van Gogh Foundation, which purchased the collection from the Van Gogh family and undertook to house it permanently in the museum.

The Dutch State, which financed the transaction and undertook to build and administer the museum.

The City of Amsterdam, which provided an extremely valuable site on Museumplein for the construction of the new museum.

POLICY

The National Museum Vincent van Gogh has the following objectives and responsibilities.

– To operate and administer the museum and its collections at state expense and in accordance with modern principles of museum management, with the aim of maintaining the museum as a living entity in the social fabric of the nation.

– To conserve the collections as if they were its own possessions.

– To place the collections on permanent public display in an artistically fitting manner.

For the next few years the exhibitions held in the museum will center on Van Gogh the artist, and will cover such topics as Van Gogh and his contem-

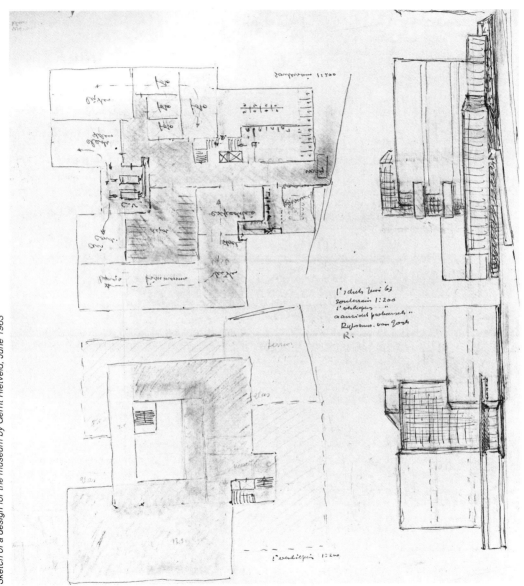

Sketch of a design for the museum by Gerrit Rietveld, June 1963

11

poraries, artistic influences on his work, his own influence on other artists, his followers, and his sources of inspiration.

Each year the museum organizes two large temporary exhibitions and a series of smaller events. Major parts of the museum's own collection remain open to the public while these events are taking place.

THE MUSEUM

In June 1963 Gerrit Rietveld produced the first sketches for the museum, working in close consultation with Dr Van Gogh. The building reproduced opposite is also by this gifted architect, who unfortunately died the following year. The design work was continued by J. van Dillen, and after his death J. van Tricht was appointed to supervise the construction of the building and the furnishing of the interor, which he had designed himself.

The Vincent van Gogh Museum opened its doors on 3 June 1973, and since then the paintings and drawings of Van Gogh and his contemporaries have drawn a steady stream of visitors.

THE VINCENT VAN GOGH FOUNDATION

The Vincent van Gogh Foundation has the following holdings, all of which are housed in the museum.
- More than 200 paintings and 500 drawings by Vincent van Gogh.
- The Theo van Gogh Collection of paintings, drawings and graphic works by Vincent's contemporaries.
- The originals of Vincent's letters to Theo.
- A collection of engravings from 19th-century illustrated magazines.
- A collection of colored Japanese woodcuts.
- An extensive archive, including press cuttings on Vincent from 1889 onwards, newspapers and periodicals.

The Foundation is also sole shareholder of BV 't Lanthuys, the publisher of the postcards, reproductions, slides, posters, etc., of the works by Van Gogh in the museum. These items are available from the museum sales desk and from certain other outlets.

THE PAINTINGS AND DRAWINGS BY VAN GOGH

The paintings are displayed in natural light in spacious, open galleries. Vincent van Gogh's drawings and his collection of Japanese prints are exhibited on a rotating basis in galleries from which daylight is excluded.

12

Theo van Gogh collected paintings, drawings and other objects by Vincent's contemporaries. Theo was 15 years old when he embarked on his career as an art dealer at the firm of Goupil & Cie. in Paris. When he died, at the age of 34, he was director of the rue Montmartre showroom of Boussod et Valadon (formerly Goupil's). He began collecting on a modest scale at an early age, and was one of the first to take an interest in the avant-garde artists of the day, whose works he exhibited in his showroom and attempted to sell to the public. Several of these artists, such as Lucien and Camille Pissarro, became his friends, and a number of the works in the collection accordingly bear an affectionate dedication.

Vincent van Gogh's arrival in Paris brought about a new relationship with the artistic community, particularly with members of the younger generation, and this intensified when he began exchanging his own works for those of his colleagues. In Paris, and later in Arles, he advised Theo on purchases which could enrich their joint collection. It is for this reason that the Theo van Gogh Collection includes paintings, watercolors, drawings and graphic works by such artists as Monticelli, Théophile de Bock, Corot, Bernard, Gauguin, Manet, Pissarro and Toulouse-Lautrec.

THE LETTERS

The letters which Vincent wrote to his brother, mother and sisters form an extremely important part of the collection, which also includes the few surviving letters from Theo to Vincent. The extant letters were published in three volumes in 1914, again thanks to the devotion of Theo's widow. In 1953 her son prepared a new edition containing numerous additional letters and documents. The letters have been translated into many languages. The extracts in this guide are from *The Complete Letters of Vincent van Gogh,* 3 vols., London 1978.

The letters which Vincent wrote in French have been published in a bibliophile facsimile edition.

The originals of the letters are stored in a special vault. In order to protect them from excessive handling they have all been photographed in full size. The reproductions can be consulted by visitors and researchers in the museum library.

THE ENGRAVINGS

Vincent van Gogh amassed a large collection of engravings from 19th-century illustrated magazines, which he refers to frequently in his letters. Almost all the engravings have been catalogued and stored on microfiche. In 1975 a selection of the English prints attracted great interest at exhibitions in England

Vincent van Gogh at the age of about 18 years

and Amsterdam. French prints from the collection were exhibited in 1972 at the Institut Néerlandais in Paris under the title *Les Sources d'Inspiration de Vincent van Gogh.*

Since the opening of the National Vincent van Gogh Museum in 1973 there have been regular exhibitions of selections from this print collection in the galleries where the drawings are displayed.

THE JAPANESE WOODCUTS

The collection of approximately 400 colored Japanese woodcuts formed by Vincent and Theo van Gogh is described in full in an illustrated catalogue published by the museum. Vincent treasured these prints, and in November 1885 he wrote to Theo from Antwerp: 'Well, one thing is sure, Antwerp is very curious and fine for a painter. My studio is not bad, especially as I have pinned a lot of Japanese prints on the wall, which amuse me very much. You know those little women's figures in gardens, or on the beach, horsemen, flowers, knotty thorn branches.' (letter 437)

The three paintings in the museum from Vincent's Paris period, the Japonaiseries *Flowering Plum Tree, Bridge in the Rain* and *The Courtesan,* are after colored woodcuts by Hiroshige and Kesai Yeisen, and express his longing for his own particular conception of the sun-drenched Far East.

ARCHIVE AND LIBRARY

The Foundation archives include numerous books and press cuttings on Vincent from 1889 onwards. They are kept in the museum library, which also serves as a reading room and study area for visitors.

The library also contains the extensive archives of Dr M.E. Tralbaut, an expert on Van Gogh, and the American collector Edward Buckman.

The unique collection of books (currently more than 10,000 volumes) is constantly being expanded under a purchasing policy which reflects the museum's overall guidelines.

The library is an indispensable research centre for art historians, visitors and students from home and abroad who wish to study 19th-century art history, and specifically the art of Vincent van Gogh.

There are also posters, exhibition and auction catalogues, modern periodicals and illustrated books.

THE VISUAL ARTS WORKSHOP

At the express wish of Dr V.W. van Gogh the museum contains an arts workshop where members of the public can learn about the visual language of art against the backdrop of Vincent's work.

Japonaiserie: The Courtesan (after Kesai Yeisen) / Paris, 2nd half of 1887   oil / canvas, 105.5 × 60.5 cm

This visual training can help to establish an interaction or dialogue between the student's own work and that of the artist. Students are taught the inter-relationship between observation, visual conception and execution by learning how to look, working from nature, and using materials and visual elements to produce compositions.

The workshop activities are listed in a programme which is published several times a year. Students' activities are supervised by seven experienced teachers who are also professional artists.

The programme includes the following elements.

- Walk-in studios, which students attend for a brief period in order to learn about artists' materials.
- Courses of twelve lessons structured to give a technical and thematic training in drawing, watercolor, painting, etching, silkscreen printing and photography.
- Work weeks, held in the museum and elsewhere approximately six times a year.

The workshop is open all year, with the exception of July. The course programmes take place in the autumn and spring, while the walk-in studios and the work weeks are generally held in the summer and winter. There is also a children's studio which is open all year with the exception of July. Programmes available on request.

OTHER FACILITIES

There is a large reproduction department where visitors can purchase books on Vincent van Gogh and his contemporaries, postcards, slides and posters. There is also a restaurant serving light refreshments. The restaurant terrace, overlooking Museum Square, is open in the summer months.

The visual arts workshop; model drawing

Throughout his career Vincent van Gogh received the loyal and loving support of his brother Theo, who helped him both financially and morally. In return Vincent sent him studies, drawings and finished paintings.

At first Theo kept Vincent's work in his Paris apartment, but eventually there were so many that he was forced to rent storage space in Julien Tanguy's art supplies shop. Tanguy was a great admirer of Van Gogh's, and gladly showed the paintings to his clients and other art-lovers. In 1888 Theo submitted three of Vincent's paintings for exhibition at the Salon des Artistes Indépendants. Further works were included in the Indépendant shows of 1889 and 1890, where they caught the eye of the critic Albert Aurier, who wrote an enthusiastic review for the *Mercure de France* in January 1890. 'Beneath skies now cut from the dazzling beauty of sapphires and turquoises, now molded from an indefinable hell—hot, stifling and blindingly yellow; beneath skies like streaming, molten metal and crystal, some with burning, radiant suns; beneath ceaseless, awesome cascades of all imaginable lights; in sulfurous, flaming, searing vapors belched forth from fantastic furnaces where gold, diamonds and rare gems are vaporized; ... there, to our alarm and consternation we see an alien nature unfold, a nature which is truly real yet almost supernatural... But let us make no mistake about it. Vincent van Gogh is by no means so far removed from his fellow countrymen... He is manifestly a Dutchman, from the illustrious line of Frans Hals.'

In 1891, after Vincent's death, Octave Mirbeau wrote a review for the *Echo de Paris* which shows that interest in Vincent's work was already growing. 'At the exhibition of the Indépendants the paintings of the deeply lamented Vincent van Gogh are causing a great stir... When one stands before these canvases, whose black mourning ribbon draws the attention of the indifferent mass of passersby, one grieves to think that this brilliantly gifted painter, this most sensitive, instinctive, visionary artist, is no more.'

In January 1891 Theo also died, and his young widow, Johanna van Gogh-Bonger, was left not only with a mass of paintings and drawings, and countless letters and prints, but above all with a baby barely a year old who had been named after his uncle, the artist Vincent van Gogh. On her return to the Netherlands she set about bringing Vincent's paintings to the attention of a wider public, bringing to her task a remarkable dedication and devotion to his memory.

In 1891 Vincent was remembered at an exhibition of Les Vingt in Brussels, and this was followed by numerous exhibitions throughout Holland. In 1892 the artist Emile Bernard, a friend of Vincent's since their student days together in 1886, succeeded in organizing a small one-man show in a Paris

Coming Out of Church in Nuenen/Nuenen, January 1884   oil/canvas, 41.5 × 32 cm

gallery just opened by Le Barc de Boutteville. In 1892 and 1893 there were retrospectives in The Hague, at the Pulchri Studio and the Haagsche Kunstkring, and in Amsterdam at the Buffa Gallery, Arti et Amicitiae and the Art Gallery of the Panorama Building. Jan Veth, the artist and critic, reviewed the Kunstkring exhibition in the *Amsterdammer* of 27 March 1892: '[that] this exhibition, however, will bring about a revelation, and that many will have the same experience as myself who, put off at first by the raw violence of some ugly Van Goghs, did not come to value the greatness in so much of his work, but who now, having grasped his beauty, accepts the man in his entirety and not merely as a rare, interesting figure.'

The artist R.N. Roland Holst had the following to say in his introduction to the Panorama exhibition of 87 paintings, 25 drawings and a number of letters. 'Exhibitions are mostly arranged not to instruct but to gratify visitors. The majority of painters are flatterers of the public taste... But art is, and always has been, the word we use to describe the higher expressions of our most precious spiritual heritage. Vincent van Gogh's expressions will certainly deter all those whose taste is usually gratified at the official exhibitions... This exhibition is assembled for those few who still believe that what is immediately grasped is not necessarily the best. It is assembled, too, for those who admire Vincent's work, and for those who already believed in his lofty search but were not convinced of his glorious achievement.'

In 1892, at the Oldenzeel Gallery in Rotterdam, Van Gogh's drawings were not only exhibited but also found buyers. Hidde Nijland, an art dealer from Dordrecht, began collecting Van Gogh, and in 1928 he sold his collection to Mrs Kröller-Müller.

In 1903 the director of the Boymans-van Beuningen Museum in Rotterdam was the first to buy a painting from Mrs Van Gogh-Bonger for inclusion in a museum. In July and August 1905 the Stedelijk Museum in Amsterdam organized a major retrospective of 474 paintings and drawings. It attracted between 25 and 30 people a day—a very meager attendance by our standards.

In France Van Gogh's paintings were commanding higher and higher prices, and it was from here that some of his finest works passed to collections in Moscow and Leningrad.

In 1893 Van Gogh and Gauguin were exhibited side by side in Copenhagen, and in 1898 other Scandinavian shows followed in Oslo, Stockholm and Gothenburg.

The art dealer Paul Cassirer became a fervent champion of Van Gogh, and in 1905 he held two retrospectives at his galleries in Hamburg and Berlin. These were the first in a long series of German exhibitions, including one at the museum in Berlin in 1906. In Cologne in 1912 a major survey of modern European art entitled *Internationale Kunstausstellung des Sonderbundes Westdeutscher Kunstfreunde und Künstler* had a profound influence on art appreciation in Germany. Interest in Vincent was further stimulated by the books of the Expressionist writer, Julius Meier-Graefe, who concluded his novel *Vincent van Gogh* with the words: 'The aim of this novel is to nourish the legend.'

From time to time extracts from Vincent's letters to his brother Theo appeared, chiefly in exhibition catalogues. In 1914 the Wereldbibliotheek Amsterdam published a virtually complete edition of the letters in three volumes, again on the initiative of the tireless Jo van Gogh-Bonger. As she wrote in the foreword to this first Dutch edition (some of the letters had already been published in France and Germany), she had deliberately avoided releasing the letters before. 'Much time was necessary to decipher the letters and to arrange them; this was the more difficult because often the dates failed, and much careful thought was needed before these letters were fitted into their place. There was another reason, however, which kept me from making them known earlier. It would have been an injustice to Vincent to create interest in his personality ere the work to which he gave his life was recognized and appreciated as it deserved. Many years passed before Vincent was recognized as a great painter. Now it is time his personality was known and understood.'

Numerous exhibitions followed, not only in the Netherlands but all over the world. The letters have been translated into many languages, and read and reread. There have been documentaries and feature films about Vincent van Gogh, and his fame and the prices paid for his paintings continue to rise. The books written about him fill an entire library, such as the one in the museum that bears his name. But the very fact that there is a Vincent van Gogh Museum, with a collection which gives such a varied, balanced picture of the artist, is due in no small part to the efforts of Dr Vincent Willem van Gogh, the son of Theo and Jo van Gogh. It is thanks to his love and determination that the collection has remained intact, and that it has found its final home in Amsterdam.

Johanna van Gogh-Bonger with her baby Vincent Willem in 1890

Theo van Gogh in Paris, 1889

Johanna van Gogh-Bonger

Still Life with Cups, Bowls and Three Bottles/Nuenen, first months of 1885   oil/canvas, 39.5 × 56 cm

Two Women Digging, and a Wheelbarrow/Drenthe, October 1883   oil/canvas, 27.5 × 36.5 cm

The Hut / Drenthe, November 1883   oil / canvas, 37.5 × 55.5 cm

Head of a Peasant Woman with White Cap/Nuenen, March 1885   oil/canvas, 43 × 33.5 cm

A Pair of Shoes/Paris, autumn 1886   oil/canvas, 37.5 × 45 cm

'My father is a clergyman in a village in Holland. I went to school when I was eleven and stayed until I was sixteen. Then I had to choose a profession, but did not know which. Through the influence of one of my uncles, partner in the firm of Goupil & Co., Art Dealers and Publishers of Engravings, I obtained a situation in this business at The Hague. I was employed there for three years. From there I went to London to learn English, and after two years I left London for Paris.' (letter 69a from *The Complete Letters of Vincent van Gogh,* 3 vols., London 1978) Vincent van Gogh wrote this brief autobiographical sketch in 1876, when he was 23 years old. Although as yet he had no inkling of what the future held, his visits to museums and exhibitions and his love of English and French literature were to have a major influence on the course of his life.

In August 1872 he wrote to his brother Theo from The Hague. This was the first in a long series of letters which Theo preserved and which were to link Vincent indissolubly with his brother, friend and spiritual refuge until his death. In them he tells Theo of his daily life, and of his experiences with nature and art.

31 May 1875, Paris: 'Yesterday I saw the Corot exhibition... At the Salon there are three very fine Corots... Of course I have also been to the Louvre and the Luxembourg... I wish you could see the little Rembrandts there, *The Men of Emmaus* and its counterpart, *The Philosophers*.' (L.27)

6 July 1875, Paris: 'I have taken a little room in Montmartre which I am sure you would like. It is small, but it overlooks a little garden full of ivy and wild vines.' (L.30) He also tells of the prints which he has on his walls, which include works by Thijs Maris, Daubigny, Corot and Millet.

24 July 1875, Paris: 'A few days ago we received a picture by De Nittis...' (L.32)

28 March 1876, Paris: 'Yesterday I saw six

Rev. Theodorus van Gogh, father of Vincent and Theo

pictures by Michel... At the same time I saw a very large picture by Jules Dupré. There is black marshy soil as far as one can see, on the second plan is a river, and in the foreground, a pool with three horses. Both the river and the pool reflect a bank of white and gray clouds, behind which the sun has set. The sky is a soft blue, with some gray-red and purple at the horizon. I saw these pictures at Durand Ruel's.' (L. 58)

In 1876 he spends a few months in England as a teacher at a boarding school, and begins to think of becoming a preacher. During this period he occasionally takes up his pencil to make drawings of his surroundings for Theo. 31 May 1876, Ramsgate: 'Enclosed is a little drawing of the view from the school window... You ought to have seen it this week when it rained, especially in the twilight when the lamps were lit and their light was reflected in the wet streets.' (L. 67)

In May 1877 he decides to follow in his father's footsteps, and goes to stay with one of his uncles in Amsterdam in order to prepare himself for the study of theology at the university. However, he finds it impossible to master the Latin and Greek he needs, and abandons his studies. He leaves Amsterdam and takes a brief course in Brussels to prepare himself for what he still sees as his life's task—to bring the gospel to the people. In the autumn of 1878 he goes to the Borinage, a mining region of Belgium, where he practises the ideal of Christian charity with fanatical zeal. In his letters to Theo, which have become more intermittent, he gives a detailed and moving account of the life of the miners. However, he has not forgotten art altogether. 'Have you seen any beautiful pictures lately? I am eager for a letter from you. Has Israëls done much lately and Maris and Mauve?' (L. 129) The letters become even fewer and far between, but then, in July 1880, he writes thanking his brother for a present of 50 francs. This marks

The art dealer Vincent van Gogh, called "Uncle Cent"

Pont de la Grande Jatte/Paris, summer 1887   oil/canvas, 32 × 40.5 cm

Woman Sitting in the Café du Tambourin/Paris, Febr./March 1887   oil/canvas, 55.5 × 46.5 cm

the start of the financial support which Theo was to give him regularly from now on, and which enabled him to become an artist. This particular letter can be regarded as the key to the philosophy by which Van Gogh, the man and the artist, lived for the next ten years.

'I am writing to you with some reluctance, not having done so in such a long time, for many reasons. To a certain degree you have become a stranger to me... At Etten I learned that you had sent 50 francs for me; well I have accepted them... So I am writing you to thank you... Now I must bore you with certain abstract things, but I hope you will listen to them patiently. I am a man of passions, capable of and subject to doing more or less foolish things, which I happen to repent, more or less, afterwards. Now and then I speak and act too hastily, when it would have been better to wait patiently. I think other people sometimes make the same mistakes... For instance, to name one of the passions, I have a more or less irresistible passion for books, and I continually want to instruct myself, to study if you like, just as much as I want to eat my bread. *You* will certainly be able to understand this. When I was in other surroundings, in the surroundings of pictures and works of art, you know how I had a violent passion for them, reaching the highest pitch of enthusiasm. And I am not sorry about it, for even now, *far from that land, I am often homesick for the land of pictures*... So you would be wrong in persisting in the belief that, for instance, I should now be less enthusiastic for Rembrandt, or Millet, or Delacroix, or whoever it may be; the contrary is true. But, you see, there are many things which one must believe and love. There is something of Rembrandt in Shakespeare, and of Correggio in Michelet, and of Delacroix in Victor Hugo... And in Bunyan there is something of Maris or of Millet, and in Beecher Stowe there is something of Ary Scheffer...

Page from a letter of Vincent to his brother Theo, July 1880, written in the Borinage (L.133)

Café ''Au Charbonnage'' at Laeken/November 1878   pencil, pen, 13.8 x 14.3 cm

"En route"/Brussels, January 1881 pen, ink, pencil, 9.7 × 5.8 cm

A caged bird in spring knows quite well that he might serve some end; he is well aware that there is something for him to do, but he cannot do it. What is it? He cannot quite remember. Then some vague idea occurs to him, and he says to himself, ''The others build their nests and lay their eggs and bring up their little ones''; and he knocks his head against the bars of the cage. But the cage remains, and the bird is maddened by anguish. ''Look at that lazy animal,'' says another bird in passing, ''he seems to be living at ease.'' Yes, the prisoner lives, he does not die; there are no outward signs of what passes within him—his health is good, he is more or less gay when the sun shines. But then the season of migration comes, and attacks of melancholia—''But he has everything he wants,'' say the children who tend him in his cage. He looks through the bars at the overcast sky where a thunderstorm is gathering, and inwardly he rebels against his fate. ''I am caged, I am caged, and you tell me I do not want anything, fools! You think I have everything I need! Oh! I beseech you liberty, that I may be a bird like other birds!'' A certain idle man resembles this idle bird.' (L.133) A month later, on 20 August 1880, he writes from Cuesmes: 'I must tell you that I am busy trying to sketch large drawings after Millet, and that I have already finished *The Four Hours of the Day* as well as *The Sower*.' (L.134) A few months later Van Gogh is hard at work drawing the human figure from Bargue's exercises and after reproductions of paintings. From the outset his drawings show an excellent grasp of composition and a remarkably individual style.

La Barrière with Horse Tramway / Paris, summer 1887   watercolor, pen, pencil, 24 × 31.5 cm

In the autumn Vincent leaves the Borinage and goes to Brussels to take drawing lessons. Here he meets Anthon van Rappard, a young artist whom Theo had known in Paris. Van Rappard offers Vincent the use of his studio in Brussels, and they enter onto a long friendship.

In the spring of 1881 Vincent returns to his parents' house in Etten in the Dutch province of North Brabant. 'I am very glad things have been arranged so that I shall be able to work here quietly for a while. I hope to make as many studies as I can, for that is the seed which must later produce the drawings,' he writes cheerfully to Theo (L.144). He finds inspiration in the Brabant countryside, which he loves. Again and again in his work we see his fascination with people who work on the land, and with the landscape where they lived out their lives. Peasants sowing, digging, hewing, their huts and the fields, the trees lining the country lanes— he draws them over and over again, constantly improving his technique. September 1881: 'I have drawn five times over a man with a spade, a Digger [un bêcheur], in different positions, a sower twice, a girl with a broom twice. Then a woman in a white cap, peeling potatoes; a shepherd leaning on his staff; and, finally, an old, sick farmer sitting on a chair near the hearth, his head in his hands and his elbows on his knees... Diggers, sowers, plowers, male and female, they are what I must draw continually. I have to observe and draw everything that belongs to country life.' (L.150) And then come his first attempts at watercolor: 'And then last week I received from Uncle in Prinsenhage a paintbox which is still very good, certainly good enough to begin on... I am very glad to have it. I at once started to make a kind of watercolor, like the sketch below.' (L.151) In December Vincent takes painting lessons in The Hague from Anton Mauve, a cousin by marriage. These are his first paintings. 'I have now painted

Peasant with Spade. Sketch in letter 150 Etten, September 1881

five studies and two watercolors and, of course, a few more sketches. I cannot tell you how kind and friendly Mauve and Jet are to me these days. And Mauve has shown and told me things which of course I cannot do at once, but which I shall gradually put into practice... The painted studies are still life, the watercolors are made after the model, a Scheveningen girl.' (L.163)

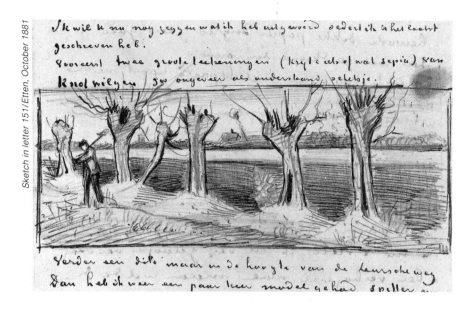

Pear Tree in Blossom/Arles, April 1888 oil/canvas, 73 × 46 cm

After an argument with his father and an unhappy love affair it becomes increasingly difficult for Vincent to stay in his parents' house, and in December 1881 he decides to rent a studio in The Hague. He is drawn to the city not only by his friendship with Mauve, who was a leading member of the Hague School, but also by his growing need for contact with other artists. Vincent had first encountered the work of the Hague School when he worked for Goupil, the art dealers. Before long, however, he falls out with Mauve, and begins mixing more with young artists such as De Bock, Van der Weele and Breitner. Vincent and Breitner discover a common interest in the latest novels by Zola and other French authors, and together they set out to draw the people and views found in the poorest quarters of The Hague. 'He [Breitner] is busy with a large picture, a market full of figures. Last night I went out with him to look for types among the people in the streets, so as to study them afterward at home with a model. In this way I made a drawing like the above of an old woman I saw on the Geest, where the insane asylum is.' (L.178)

Corner of Herengracht and Prinsessegracht in The Hague
The Hague, March 1882   pencil, washed with China ink,
heightened with white, 24 × 33.9 cm

Vincent's technique and skill are advancing rapidly, so much so that his Uncle Cor, an art dealer in Amsterdam, orders twelve drawings of The Hague. Vincent is delighted with his first commission, and charges Dfl. 2.50 a drawing. A second commission for six drawings follows.

Shortly after his arrival in the city Vincent starts collecting prints from English and French magazines, particularly sheets by artists like Holl, Herkomer and Fildes. He decides to follow their example and make drawings as studies for lithographs which could be used as illustrations. He gives shelter to a pregnant prostitute called Sien, probably prompted by his interest in social themes and his identification with the lot of the poor. Other motives for entering onto this relationship, which deeply offended his friends, were his longing for a family life, for Sien already had a daughter and there was the baby to come, and the constant availability of a model. One of his most moving and sublime drawings is *Sorrow,* of which he also makes a lithograph.

In the summer of 1882 he starts working seriously in oils. Up until now he has only used them sporadically, because he wanted to become proficient in drawing first. In his letters of 5 and 6 August he describes his palette to Theo, and tells him about a perspective frame which he has designed after the example of Leonardo da Vinci and Dürer. He continued to use this frame for a long time, and traces of it can be seen in some of his drawings.

41

Orphan Man with Walking Stick, Seen from the Back/The Hague, September/December 1882   pencil, 47.5 × 26 cm

Orphan Man with Walking Stick/The Hague, September/December 1882   pencil, 50 × 30.5 cm

Plowman and Two Women on a Potato Field. Sketch in letter 333/Drenthe, October 1883

DRENTHE AND BRABANT

In the autumn of 1883 he can no longer stand the mental and financial pressure from Sien and her family and leaves The Hague, abandoning a large number of studies. He goes to Drenthe, in the north of Holland, in search of inspiration. This is a brief but important period in his development, and lasts from September to December 1883. It is a search for new images, a return to rural themes in imitation of other artists, like his friend Van Rappard, who had also visited this windswept, monotonous and impoverished region. Van Gogh rediscovers his peasants, their huts, and their labors on the land, although in Drenthe they are peat workers. Now, though, he sees them with the eyes of an artist, and his style is different. Here, in the flat Drenthe countryside, he finds echoes not only of the artists of the Barbizon School but also of 17th-century Dutch landscape art. From Nieuw Amsterdam he writes: 'This once I write to you from the very remotest part of Drenthe, where I came after an endless expedition on a barge through the moors. I see no possibility of describing the country as it ought to be done; words fail me, but imagine the banks of the canal as miles and miles of Michels or Th. Rousseaus, Van Goyens or Ph. de Konincks. Level planes or strips of different color, getting narrower and narrower as they approach the horizon. Accentuated here and there by a peat shed or small farm, or a few meager birches, poplars, oaks—heaps of peat everywhere... The figures which now and then appear on the plain are generally of an impressive character.' (L.330)

In December Vincent visits his parents in Nuenen, the village to which his father has been appointed. He only plans to stay a short while, but then changes his mind and does not return to Drenthe. 'Drenthe is splendid, but one's being able to stay there depends on many things, depends on whether one is able to stand the loneliness.' (L.344)

The Weaver: The Whole Loom, Facing Left/Nuenen, February 1884   pen, 12.6 × 19.7 cm

Van Gogh remains two years in Nuenen, working on paintings and drawings of the Brabant countryside, with its houses and churches, and of the peasants and weavers living in and around the village.

He writes to Van Rappard: 'A few days ago I sent you three more pen-and-ink drawings, *Little Ditch, Norway Pines in the Fen, Thatched Roofs;* I thought you would like the subjects. As for the execution, I should have wished with all my heart that the direction of the pen scratches had followed the forms more expressively, and that the forces which render the tone of the masses expressed their shape more clearly at the same time... but I had to take a shot at it in a rough sort of way in order to render the effect of light and brown— the atmosphere of the scenery as it was at that moment—the general aspect—as well as I could.' (L.R45)

He is clearly preoccupied with themes and techniques which can also be found in the paintings and drawings from his French period. One example is his painting of the tower of Nuenen church, with its broken spire and the crows flying around the empty windows, which in its force can well be compared to his painting of the church at Auvers. His second important group of works, of the people of Brabant, culminantes in his painting *The Potato Eaters.* Vincent's interest in the local weavers is not restricted to them as a picturesque subject, but also extends to the loom itself. In April 1884 he tells Van Rappard: 'As for the weaving loom, the study of that apparatus was indeed made on the spot from start to finish, and it was a hard job—on account of the fact that one must sit so close to it that it is difficult to take measurements; I did include the figure in the drawing after all... When I had finished drawing the apparatus pretty carefully, I thought it was so disgusting

Vase with Sunflowers/Arles, January 1889   oil/canvas, 95 × 73 cm

that I couldn't hear it rattle that I let the spook appear in it.' (L.R44)

In the winter of 1884 Vincent begins painting and drawing a series of portraits as studies for a composition of peasants in their hut. Some of these portraits are moving evocations of old age and lives devoted to hard, manual labor. To Theo: 'I am very busy painting those heads. I paint in the daytime and draw in the evening. In this way I have already painted at least some thirty and drawn as many.' (L.394) In his next letter: 'Just now I paint not only as long as there is daylight, but even in the evening by the lamp in the cottages, when I can hardly distinguish anything on my palette, so as to catch, if possible, something of the curious effects of lamplight, with, for instance, a large shadow cast on the wall.' (L.395)

In April he sums up his ideas for *The Potato Eaters*. 'All winter long I have the threads of this tissue in my hands, and have searched for the ultimate pattern; and though it has become a tissue of rough, coarse aspect, nevertheless the threads have been carefully chosen and according to certain rules. And it might prove to be a real *peasant picture. I know it is.* But he who prefers to see the peasants in their Sunday-best may do as he likes. I personally am convinced I get better results by painting them in their roughness than by giving them a conventional charm. I think a peasant girl is more beautiful than a lady, in her dusty, patched blue skirt and bodice, which get the most delicate hues from weather, wind and sun. But if she puts on a lady's dress, she loses her peculiar charm. A peasant is more real in his fustian clothes in the fields than when he goes to church on Sunday in a kind of dress coat. In the same way it would be wrong, I think, to give a peasant picture a certain conventional smooth-ness. If a peasant picture smells of bacon, smoke, potato steam—all right, that's not unhealthy; if a

Head of a Peasant Woman: Right Profile/Nuenen, May/June 1885   black chalk, 40 × 33 cm

The Old Church Tower at Nuenen/Nuenen, May 1885   oil/canvas, 63 × 79 cm

Study of Three Hands, Two of Them with a Fork/Nuenen, April 1885   black chalk, charcoal, 20 x 33 cm

stable smells of dung—all right, that belongs to
a stable; if the field has an odor of ripe corn or
potatoes or of guano or manure—that's healthy,
especially for city people.' (L.404)
Vincent's father, the Reverend Theodorus van
Gogh, dies suddenly on 26 March 1885. Vincent
is deeply affected. In October he paints 'a still life
of an open—so a broken white—Bible bound in
leather, against a black background, with yellow-
brown foreground, with a touch of citron yellow.'
(L. 429) Beside the Bible stands a burned-out candle.
Difficulties with the priest and the people of
Nuenen prevent him from getting any more models,
and at the end of the summer he decides to leave.
Besides, he is becoming more and more intrigued
by Theo's stories of the new methods being
used by French artists. One of his letters to Theo

contains a detailed analysis of color theories
based on Delacroix. He is obviously exploring
new impulses for his art, and wants to broaden his
horizons. In November he departs for Antwerp.
'As to my feeling the loss of a studio in Antwerp,
yes, I certainly shall. But I must choose between
a studio without work here, and work without a
studio there.' (L.435)

The Zouave/Arles, June 1888   oil/canvas, 65 × 54 cm

Women Dancing/Antwerp, December 1885   black (charcoal?) and colored chalk, 9.4 × 16.4 cm

In mid-November Vincent had told Theo that he was longing to go to Antwerp, and that the first thing he planned to do was go and see the paintings of the Belgian artist Leys. 'I imagine it will be beautiful there this winter, especially the docks with snow.' (L. 434) He will also be taking some of the paintings he is working on. 'The one landscape I am taking with me . . . the one with the yellow leaves, I believe you would like too. I am enclosing a hasty scratch of it. The horizon is a dark streak against a light streak of sky in white and blue. In that dark streak, little patches of red, bluish and green, or brown, forming the silhouette of the roofs and orchards, the field greenish. The sky higher up, gray, with the black saplings and yellow leaves against it. The foreground all covered with yellow leaves, in which are two little black figures and a blue one. To the right, a birch trunk, white and black, and a green trunk with red-brown leaves.' (L. 434)

Another reason for going to Antwerp was the chance of seeing a large collection of work by Rubens. 'Rubens is certainly making a strong impression on me; I think his drawing tremendously good—I mean the drawing of heads and hands in themselves. I am quite carried away by his way of drawing the lines in a face with streaks of pure red, or of modeling the fingers of the hands by the same kind of streaks. I go to the museum fairly often, and then I look at little else but a few heads and hands of his and of Jordaens'.' (L. 439) At first Vincent is happier in Antwerp, as can be seen from his sketches. Not only does his palette become lighter, but he is also less melancholy. 'Antwerp is beautiful in color, and it is worth while just for the subjects. One evening I saw a popular sailors' ball at the docks; it was most interesting and they behaved *quite decently* . . . There were several very handsome girls, the most beautiful of

Registration form of Vincent van Gogh for the Academy of Antwerp

whom was plain-faced…, one in black silk… who danced perfectly in an old-fashioned style. Once she danced with a well-to-do little farmer who carried a big green umbrella under his arm, even when he waltzed very quickly.' (L. 438)

In January 1886 Vincent enrolls at the Antwerp academy in order to develop his technique of painting and drawing from the model under trained teachers. It ends in fiasco, although he does write: 'I want to tell you that Verlat has at last seen my work… so tomorrow I shall start working in the academy's painting class.' (L. 445) But this is soon followed by letters in which he urges Theo to let him come to Paris. 'So please allow me to come sooner, I should almost say at once. If I rent a garret in Paris, and bring my paintbox and drawing materials with me, then I can finish what is most pressing at once—those studies from the ancients, which certainly will help me a great deal when I go to Cormon's [a well-known Paris studio].' (L. 452)

Towards the end of his time in Antwerp Vincent's health is giving cause for concern, and he is having trouble with his teeth. 'For the rest, it is only natural that there cannot be any objection to finding a garret in Paris at once, on the very first day of my arrival, and then I can go and draw at the Louvre or the Ecole des Beaux-Arts… So if it were at all possible, I should like to have that job on my teeth finished this month. I should like to pack up my studies and send them to you, and then leave here on the last of this month, or even a few days sooner.' (L. 455)

Without waiting for Theo's agreement Vincent arrives unexpectedly in Paris at the beginning of March. A messenger brings Theo the following pencilled note: 'Do not be cross with me for having come all at once like this; I have thought about it so much, and I believe that in this way we shall save time. Shall be at the Louvre from midday on or sooner if you like. Please let me know at what time

cont. p. 56   **51**

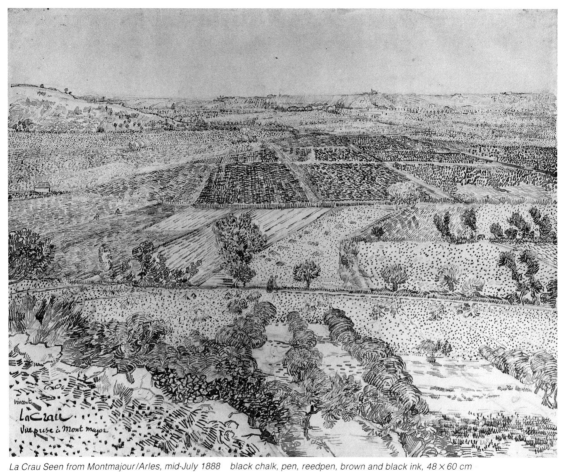

La Crau Seen from Montmajour/Arles, mid-July 1888   black chalk, pen, reedpen, brown and black ink, 48 × 60 cm

Harvest at La Crau/Arles, June 1888   oil/canvas, 73 × 92 cm

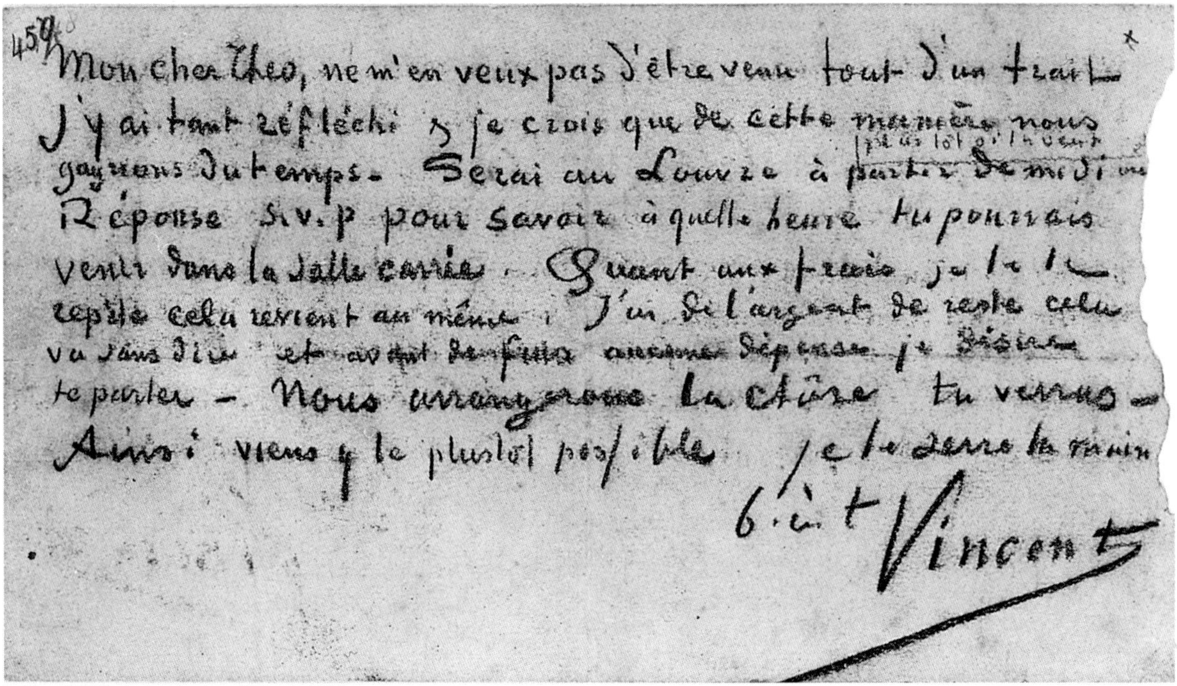

459

Mon cher Theo, ne m'en veux pas d'être venu tout d'un trait.
J'y ai tant réfléchi & je crois que de cette manière nous
gagnerons du temps. Serai au Louvre à partir de midi ou
Réponse s.v.p pour savoir à quelle heure tu pourrais
venir dans la Salle carrée. Quant aux frais je te le
répète cela revient au même. J'ai de l'argent de reste cela
va sans dire et avant de faire aucune dépense je désire
te parler — Nous arrangerons la chose tu verras —
Ainsi viens y le plus tôt possible. je te serre la main

b. à t. Vincent

Letter 459/Paris, beginning of March 1886

54

The Clarinettist and Flutist / Paris, summer 1886   blue chalk, 26 × 35 cm

The Banks of the Seine at Paris/Paris, early 1886   pencil, 10.9 × 19.8 cm

you could come to the Salle Carrée. As for the
expenses, I tell you again, this comes to the same
thing. I have some money left, of course, and I
want to speak to you before I spend any of it. We'll fix
things up, you'll see. So, come as soon as possible.
I shake your hand.' (L.459)

During his two years in Paris Van Gogh is flooded
with so many new experiences, both visual and
social, that it almost becomes too much for him.
He moves in to Theo's small apartment in the rue
Laval. Since there is no room for a studio he often
wanders through the city, sketchpad in hand,
revisiting the spots he had known before. He goes
to museums and exhibitions, and under Theo's
influence he begins leading a more regular life.
Together with Theo's friend, Andries Bonger, they
eat each day at Montmartre restaurants, and on
some evenings the three young men visit nearby
cabarets, such as the Chat Noir.

Theo's apartment is really too small for two
people, so the brothers soon move to a larger home
with room for a studio in the rue Lepic, also in
Montmartre. There Vincent throws himself into
his work, and his health improves. In June 1886
Theo writes to their mother: 'You wouldn't
recognize Vincent, he has changed so much.
Others notice it even more than I do... The doctor
says that he is now perfectly fit again. He is
making tremendous strides with his work, and the
proof of it is that he is beginning to achieve
success. He hasn't yet sold any canvases, but
exchanges them for other paintings. We're
beginning to build up a fine collection in this way,
and it's worth something too, of course. There is a
picture dealer who has already taken four of his
paintings in this way and has promised to hold an
exhibition of his work next year. Mostly he paints
flowers, in order to get fresher colors into his next

The Sower / Arles, end of November 1888   oil / canvas, 32 × 40 cm

The Terrace of the Tuileries/Paris, early 1886   pencil, 9.8 × 15.8 cm

paintings. He is also far livelier than he used to be, and is popular with people.' Theo also writes to an old friend in The Hague, Mrs Van Stockum-Haanebeek, telling her about their apartment.
'As you may know I am now living with my brother Vincent, who is studying the art of painting with indefatigable zeal. As he requires rather a lot of space for his work, we are living in a rather big apartment in Montmartre, which is, as you know, a suburb of Paris, built on the slope of a hill. The remarkable thing about our dwelling is that one has a magnificent view of the whole town from its windows, with the hills of Meudon, St. Cloud and so on on the horizon, and over it an expanse of sky nearly as large as when one is standing on the top of a dune. With the different effects produced by the various changes in the sky it is a subject for I don't know how many pictures.' (L.T1a) Theo has been promoted head of the Boussod et

Valadon gallery (formerly Goupil & Cie.) in the Boulevard Montmartre, where he also exhibits works by avant-garde artists who were unsaleable at the time, and it is here that Vincent meets impressionists like Claude Monet and Edgar Degas. In the studio of the painter Cormon, where Vincent takes lessons for a while, he also gets to know younger artists such as Emile Bernard, Henri de Toulouse-Lautrec, and the Australian, John Russell. From Paris Vincent writes to H.M. Levens, an Englishman with whom he had lived and worked for a time in Antwerp: 'Since I am here in Paris I have very often thought of yourself and work. You will remember that I liked your colour, your ideas on art and literature and I add, most of all your personality... There is much to be seen here— for instance Delacroix, to name only one master. In Antwerp I did not even know what the impressionists were, now I have seen them and though *not*

View of Paris with the Opera/Paris, summer or autumn 1886   black pencil, white and brownish-red chalk, 22.5 × 30 cm

Le Père Tanguy/Paris, late 1887   pencil, 21.5 × 13.5 cm

being one of the club yet I have much admired certain impressionists' pictures—*Degas* nude figures—*Claude Monet* landscape. And now for what regards what I myself have been doing, I have lacked money for paying models else I had entirely given myself to figure painting. But I have made a series of color studies in painting, simply flowers, red poppies, blue corn flowers and myosotys, white and rose roses, yellow chrysanthemums—seeking oppositions of blue with orange, red and green, yellow and violet: *les tons rompus et neutres* to harmonise brutal extremes.' (L.459a)

Needless to say, while they are living together Vincent only writes when Theo is out of town, as he generally is in the summer, when he goes to Holland. In 1887 Vincent had become the lover of Agostina Segatori, an Italian woman who ran the artists' café Le Tambourin. That summer he tells Theo about the break-up of the relationship. 'As for the Segatori, that's very different. I still have some affection for her, and I hope she still has some for me. But just now she is in a bad way; she is neither a free agent nor mistress in her own house... I saw Tanguy yesterday, and he has put a canvas I've just done in his window. I have done four since you left, and am working on a big one. I know that these big long canvases are difficult to sell, but later on people will see that there is open air in them and good humor.' (L.462)

Accompanied by friends like Bernard and Signac, Vincent goes on painting excursions outside Paris: to Asnières, where Bernard lives, along the Seine, to the quarries outside Montmartre, and by horse-drawn tram to the city ramparts. He also paints portraits, as Theo tells their mother: 'He has painted one or two portraits which have turned out well, but he *will* work for nothing. It is a pity that he shows no desire to earn some money, because he could easily do so here; but one cannot change people.'

Self-portrait with Straw Hat / Paris, summer 1887   oil / pasteboard, 40.5 × 32.5 cm

This Paris period provided Vincent with a wealth of influences—stylistic, coloristic and innovative—which he wove into his *œuvre* to create a highly personal style. His color sense now comes to full maturity, but he is so overwhelmed by all these impressions and discoveries that he begins to long for somewhere quieter to work, so that he can absorb them properly. It also has to be somewhere warm and sunny, where he can paint out of doors the whole year round. He writes to his sister: 'If I did not have Theo, it would not be possible for me to get what I have a right to; but seeing that he is my friend, I believe I shall make still further progress, and give free rein to it. It is my intention as soon as possible to go temporarily to the South, where there is even more color, even more sun... And when I was painting landscapes at Asnières last summer, I saw more color in it than before.' (L.W1) He finally chooses Arles in Provence, and on Sunday 19 February 1888 he leaves Paris. 'During the journey I thought of you at least as much as I did of the new country I was seeing. Only I said to myself that perhaps later on you will often be coming here yourself. It seems to me almost impossible to work in Paris unless one has some place of retreat where one can recuperate and get one's tranquility and poise back. Without that, one would get hopelessly stultified,' he tells Theo after arriving in Arles. (L.463)

Boulevard de Clichy/Paris, February/March 1887   pen, blue, pink and white chalk, 38 × 52.5 cm

Japonaiserie: The Flowering Plum Tree (after Hiroshige) / Paris, 1st half of 1887   oil/canvas, 55 × 46 cm

In Arles Van Gogh rents a room near the station.
Although there has been an unexpected fall of
snow and it is really quite cold, he feels more
optimistic and healthy than he had in Paris. He
immediately starts exploring the town and its
surroundings, and begins painting with the aid of
his perspective frame, which he had first used back
in The Hague. The correspondence with his
brother picks up again, and the many letters
provide an almost day-to-day record of his life
and work in Arles.
'Here I am seeing new things, I am learning, and if
I take it easy, my body doesn't refuse to function...
I made my last three studies with the perspective
frame I told you about, I attach some importance to
the use of the frame because it seems not unlikely
to me that in the near future many artists will
make use of it, just as the old German and Italian
painters certainly did, and, as I am inclined to think,
the Flemish too.' (L.469)
Spring arrives, and he begins painting the flowering
orchards with unflagging enthusiasm. In his
mind's eye he sees his canvases hanging on the
wall like triptychs. 'You see from the three
squares on the other side of this page that the three
orchards make a series, more or less. I have also
just now a little pear tree, vertical, between two
horizontal canvases... You see, we may consider
this year's nine canvases as the first design for a
final scheme of decoration a great deal bigger...
Here is the other middle piece of the size 12
canvases. The ground violet, in the background
a wall with straight poplars and a very blue sky.
The little pear tree has a violet trunk and white
flowers, with a big yellow butterfly on one of the
clusters. To the left in the corner, a little garden
with a fence of yellow reeds, and green bushes,
and a flower bed. A little pink house'. (L.477)
He has long wanted to have a house with a studio
where he can work in peace and put up friends

*The Flowering Tree/Arles, March 1888   charcoal, black chalk
and watercolor, 45.5 × 30.5 cm*

The Yellow House/Arles, end of September 1888   oil/canvas, 72 × 91.5 cm

Orchard in the Provence/Arles, April 1888   pencil, reed pen, white and pink gouache, 39.5 × 54 cm

who want to come and stay. Finally, not far from Arles Station, he finds the 'yellow house', which stands on a square facing a park with the River Rhône flowing close by. On 1 May, Theo's birthday, he writes: 'You will find among them a hasty sketch on yellow paper, a lawn in the square as you come into the town, with a building at the back, rather like this:—. Well, today I've taken the right wing of this complex, which contains 4 rooms, or rather two with two cabinets. It is painted yellow outside, whitewashed inside, on the sunny side. I have taken it for 15 fr. a month... And after this I can venture to tell you that I mean to invite Bernard and others to send me pictures, to show them here if there is an opportunity... I shall see my canvases in a bright interior—the floor is red brick; outside, the garden of the square, of which you will find two more drawings.' (L. 480)

But Van Gogh wants to do more than exhibit the works of his friends in Arles. His dream is to found a community where artists can work together and stimulate each other. The first one he approaches is a friend from his Paris days, Paul Gauguin.

In 1888 Gauguin is working in Brittany, but is in poor health and is having financial problems. All year Vincent prepares for Gauguin's arrival, and furnishes the 'yellow house' for him. 'For a visitor there will be the prettier room upstairs, which I shall try to make as much as possible like the boudoir of a really artistic woman.' (L. 534) On the furnishing of his own bedroom he writes: 'At last I can send you a little sketch to give you at least an idea of the way the work is shaping up... This time it's just simply my bedroom, only here color is to do every-thing, and giving by its simplification a grander style to things, is to be suggestive here of *rest* or of sleep in general. In a word, looking at the picture ought to rest the brain, or rather the imagination. The walls are pale violet. The floor is of red tiles. The wood of the bed and chairs is the yellow of

Orchard with View of Arles/Arles, April 1889   oil/canvas, 50.5 × 65 cm

fresh butter, the sheets and pillows very light greenish-citron. The coverlet scarlet. The window green. The toilet table orange, the basin blue. The doors lilac... Portraits on the walls, and a mirror and a towel and some clothes.' (L.554)

His letters tell of his fascination with the landscape of Provence, and of the way in which the light and colors of the south are influencing his painting. 'For instance, there is a rough sketch I made of myself laden with boxes, props and canvas on the sunny road to Tarascon. There is a view of the Rhône in which the sky and the water are the color of absinthe, with a blue bridge and figures of little black urchins... Just now I am working on a study like this, of boats seen from the quay above, the two boats are pink tinged with violet, the water is bright green, no sky, a tricolor on the mast.' (L.524)

'Since seven o'clock this morning I have been sitting in front of something which after all is no great matter, a clipped round bush of cedar or cypress growing amid grass... The bush is green, touched a little with bronze and various other tints. The grass is bright, bright green, malachite touched with citron, and the sky is bright, bright blue. The row of bushes in the background are all oleanders, raving mad; the blasted things are flowering so riotously that they may well catch locomotor ataxia. They are loaded with fresh flowers, and quantities of faded flowers as well, and their green is continually renewing itself in fresh, strong shoots, apparently inexhaustibly. A funereal cypress is standing over them, and some small figures are sauntering along a pink path.' (L.541)

'Enclosed a little sketch of a square size 30 canvas, the starry sky actually painted at night under a gas jet. The sky is greenish-blue, the water royal blue, the ground mauve. The town is blue and violet, the gas is yellow and the reflections are russet-gold down to greenish-

Vincent's House at Arles/Arles, September/October 1888
chalk, pen, brown ink and watercolor, heightened with white,
24.5 × 30.5 cm

The Bedroom/Arles, October 1888   oil/canvas, 72 × 90 cm

Le Pont de Trinquetaille. Sketch in letter 552/October 1888

bronze. On the blue-green expanse of sky the Great Bear sparkles green and pink, its discreet pallor contrasts with the harsh gold of the gas. Two colorful little figures of lovers in the foreground.' (L.543)

'But the autumn still continues to be so beautiful! It's a queer place, this native land of Tartarin's! Yes, I am content with my lot... Now imagine an immense pine tree of greenish blue, spreading its branches horizontally over a bright green lawn, and gravel splashed with light and shade. Two figures of lovers in the shade of the great tree: size 30 canvas. This very simple patch of garden is brightened by beds of geraniums, orange in the distance under the black branches. Then two more size 30 canvases, the Trinquetaille bridge and another bridge, along the road where the railroad is.' (L.552)

Gauguin finally arrives to stay at the 'yellow house' at the end of October. The collaboration between Vincent and Gauguin is short-lived, for their ideas on art and artists are so different that they find impossible to get along together. Gauguin's influence can be seen in Vincent's symbolic painting, *Memory of the Garden at Etten,* about which he writes to his sister: 'I have just finished painting, to put in my bedroom, a memory of the garden at Etten; here is a scratch of it... Here are the details of the colors. The younger of the two ladies who are out for a walk is wearing a Scottish shawl with green and orange checks, and a red parasol. The old lady has a violet shawl, nearly black. But a bunch of dahlias, some of them citron yellow, the others pink and white mixed, are like an explosion of color on the somber figure... I know this is hardly what one might call a likeness, but for me it renders the poetic character and the style of the garden as I feel it. All the same, let us suppose that the two ladies out for a walk are you and our mother; let us even suppose that there is not the

Park with Fence/Arles, 19 September or shortly later pencil, pen, reed pen and brown ink, 32 x 24 cm

least, absolutely not the least vulgar and fatuous resemblance—yet the deliberate choice of color, the somber violet with the blotch of violent citron yellow of the dahlias, suggests Mother's personality to me. The figure in the Scotch plaid with orange and green checks stands out against the somber green of the cypress, which contrast is further accentuated by the red parasol—this figure gives me an impression of you...' (L.W9)

A visit to the museum at Montpellier leads to heated discussions between Vincent and Gauguin which end in arguments about art and artists. By December the tension reaches such a pitch that Vincent, in a fit of rage, threatens Gauguin with a knife, and then cuts off part of his own ear. Gauguin is so shocked that he immediately packs up and leaves Arles. Vincent is taken to hospital, but he recovers quickly and returns home at the beginning of January. He throws himself into his work again, but in February he is readmitted to hospital after a depressive collapse. Even there he carries on painting and drawing. He is discharged again in March, but the inhabitants of Arles have come to regard him as a kind of madman after the incident with Gauguin, and make it impossible for him to carry on working in the town. After discussions with the local vicar, the Reverend Salles, Vincent agrees to go voluntarily to the sanatorium at Saint-Rémy.

In April he writes to his friend Signac: 'At present I am well, and I work at the sanatorium and its environs. I have just come back with two studies of orchards. Here is a crude sketch of them—the big one is a poor landscape with little cottages, blue skyline of the Alpine foothills, sky white and blue... The other landscape is nearly all green with a little lilac and gray—on a rainy day.' (L.583b)

In Amsterdam, on 18 April, Theo marries Johanna Bonger, the sister of his old friend Andries. On 22 April Vincent writes: 'You will probably be back

Souvenir of the Garden at Etten. Sketch in letter W9 to Vincent's sister, Willemien/early December 1888

Wheatfield with a Reaper/Saint-Rémy, July 1889   oil/canvas, 73 × 92 cm

Window of Vincent's studio at Saint Paul's Hospital in Saint-Rémy/Saint-Rémy, May/early June 1889   black chalk, gouache, 61 × 47 cm

in Paris at the moment when this letter arrives. I wish you and your wife a great deal of happiness... At the end of the month I should like to go to the hospital in Saint-Rémy, or another institution of this kind, of which M. Salles has told me... It will be enough, I hope, if I tell you that I feel quite unable to take a new studio and to stay there alone—here in Arles or elsewhere... I should be afraid of losing the power to work, which is coming back to me now, by forcing myself and by having all the other responsibilities of a studio on my shoulders besides. And temporarily I wish to remain shut up as much for my own peace of mind as for other people's.' (L.585)

To his sister Wil: 'Mother will doubtless be pleased with Theo's marriage... As for myself, I am going to an asylum in Saint-Rémy, not far from here, for three months. I have had in all four great crises, during which I didn't in the least know what I said, what I wanted and what I did... I still feel incapable of taking a new studio. Notwithstanding this I am working, and I have just finished two pictures of the hospital, one of the ward, a very long ward, with rows of beds with white curtains, in which some figures of patients are moving... And then, as a pendant, the inner court. It is an arcaded gallery like those one finds in Arab buildings, all whitewashed. In front of those galleries an antique garden with a pond in the middle, and eight flower beds, forget-me-nots, Christmas roses, anemones, ranunculus, wall-flowers, daisies and so on. And under the gallery orange trees and oleander. So it is a picture quite full of flowers and vernal green. However, three gloomy black tree trunks pass through it like serpents, and in the foreground four big dismal clusters of somber box shrub.' (L.W11)

At first Vincent feels much calmer in the asylum at Saint-Rémy, and his urge to draw and paint is as strong as ever. He also comes to see Gauguin as

The Rock of Montmajour/Arles, July 1888   pencil, pen, reed pen, brush and black ink, 49 × 61 cm

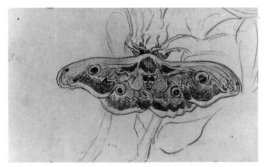

Death's-head Moth/Saint-Rémy, May 1889 black chalk, pen, brown ink, washed, 15 × 24.5 cm

The Courtyard of the Hospital in Arles/Arles, April/May 1889 pencil, reed pen and brown ink (or sepia), 45.5 × 59 cm

a friend and master again, and advises Theo to exchange paintings with him. 'If he will accept it, give Gauguin the copy of *La Berceuse*... But if Gauguin wants the sunflowers, it is only fair that he should give you something you like equally well in exchange... When I send you the four canvases of the garden I am working on, you will see that, considering my life is spent mostly in the garden, it is not so unhappy. Yesterday I drew a very big, rather rare night moth, called the death's head, its coloring of amazing distinction, black, gray, cloudy white tinged with carmine or vaguely shading off into olive-green; it is very big.' (L.592)

Until midsummer Vincent's health improves daily, and he finds endless inspiration in the beautiful countryside around the asylum, which is housed in an old monastery. 'Many thanks for the package of canvases, brushes, tobacco and chocolate which reached me in good condition. I was very glad of them, for I was feeling a little low after working. ... My health is all right, considering; I feel happier here with my work than I could be outside.' (L.594)

And a few days later: 'We have had some glorious days, and I have set even more canvases going... I have a wheatfield, very yellow and very light, perhaps the lightest canvas I have done. The cypresses are always occupying my thoughts, I should like to make something of them like the canvases of the sunflowers, because it astonishes me that they have not yet been done as I see them. It is as beautiful of line and proportion as an Egyptian obelisk... I think that of the two canvases of cypresses, the one I am making this sketch of will be the best. The trees in it are very big and massive. The foreground very low with brambles and brushwood. Behind some violet hills, a green and pink sky with a crescent moon. The foreground especially is painted very thick, clumps of brambles with touches of yellow, violet and green.' (L.596)

Olive Trees with Pink Sky/Saint-Rémy, autumn 1889   oil/canvas, 73 × 92 cm

Cypress. Sketch in letter 596/Saint-Rémy, 25 June 1889

In July 1889: 'I am sending you enclosed a sketch of the cicadas here. Their song in the great heat here has the same charm for me as the cricket on the hearth for the peasants at home.' (L.603) However, he suffers a relapse which prevents him from working outside the asylum for a while, and he has to content himself with painting copies after prints by Millet and other artists, and making portraits of the people around him. 'For many days *my mind has been absolutely wandering,* as in Arles... This new attack, my boy, came on me in the fields, on a windy day, when I was busy painting.' (L.601)

'Yesterday I began to work a little again—on a thing I see from my window—a field of yellow stubble that they are plowing, the contrast of the violet-tinted plowed earth with the strips of yellow stubble, background of hills.' (L.602)

Writing to his sister Wil, he says: 'These last weeks I have also painted some pictures for myself—I don't especially lik̂ to see my own pictures in my bedroom, which is why I copied one picture by Delacroix and some others by Millet. The Delacroix is a ''Pietà'', that is to say the dead Christ with the Mater Dolorosa. The exhausted corpse lies on the ground in the entrance of a cave, the hands held before it on the left side, and the woman is behind it. It is the evening after a thunderstorm, and that forlorn figure in blue clothes—the loose clothes are agitated by the wind—is sharply outlined against a sky in which violet clouds with golden edges are floating. She too stretches out her empty arms before her in a large gesture of despair, and one sees the good sturdy hands of a working woman. The shape of this figure with its streaming clothes is nearly as broad as it is high. And the face of the dead man is in the shadow—but the pale head of the woman stands out clearly against a cloud—a contrast which causes those two heads to seem like one somber-hued flower

Wheatfields and Cypresses / Saint-Rémy, June / July 1889   black chalk, pencil, pen, reed pen and brown ink, 47 × 62.5 cm

Pietà (after Delacroix)/Saint-Rémy, September 1889
oil/canvas, 73 × 60.5 cm

and one pale flower, arranged in such a way as mutually to intensify their effect.' (L.W14)
In September he writes to Theo: 'I have now seven copies of the ten of Millet's *Travaux des Champs*. I can assure you that making copies interests me enormously, and it means that I shall not lose sight of the figure, even though I have no models at the moment. Besides, this will make a studio decoration for me or someone else... You will be surprised at the effect *Les Travaux des Champs* takes on in color, it is a very profound series of his.' (L.607)
In the winter of 1889 the two brothers begin discussing the possibility of Vincent leaving the asylum of Saint-Rémy and finding a more congenial home. In the meantime Vincent's paintings have been shown at exhkbitions of the Indépendants at Paris and the Vingtistes in Brussels, and are beginning to attract attention. In Brussels one of his paintings is bought by the artist Anna Boch, and the critic Albert Aurier writes a glowing review. Finally Theo finds a new home for Vincent in Auvers-sur-Oise, near Paris.
A son is born to Theo and Jo van Gogh in January 1890, and is named after Vincent, who immediately begins painting a beautiful picture for his young namesake. 'A day or two ago I started painting a picture for him of a blue sky with branches full of blossoms standing out against it. It is possible that I shall see him soon—at least I hope so—toward the end of March.' (L.W20)
In May 1890 the time comes for Vincent to leave Provence: 'As for me, I can't go on, I am at the end of my patience, my dear brother... My work is going well, I have done two canvases of the fresh grass in the park, one of which is extremely simple, here is a hasty sketch of it. The trunk of a pine violet-pink and then the grass with white flowers and dandelions, a little rose tree and other tree trunks in the background right at the top of

The Sheaf-binder / Saint-Rémy, September 1889   oil / canvas, 44 × 32.5 cm

Branch of an Almond Tree in Blossom/Saint-Rémy,
February 1890   oil/canvas, 73.5 × 92 cm

the canvas. ... My surroundings here begin to
weigh on me more than I can say—my word I have
been patient for more than a year—I need air,
I feel overwhelmed with boredom and grief...
I will have myself accompanied as far as Tarascon—
even one or two stations farther if you insist, once
in Paris... you could come and meet me at the
Gare de Lyon.' (L.631)

Peasant Woman Binding Sheaves (after Millet) / Saint-Rémy, September 1889   oil/canvas on pasteboard, 43 x 33 cm

The Town Hall of Auvers-sur-Oise/Auvers, July 1890
(detail from sheet 48 × 31 cm) black chalk, 24 × 31 cm

On his way to Auvers Vincent spends three days in Paris, where he meets Theo's young wife for the first time, and sees his nephew. He is also reunited with some of his old artist friends, and sees his own paintings and drawings hanging on the walls of Theo's apartment, where they take up every inch of space. It is a tense, tiring and emotional three days, both for Vincent and for Johanna van Gogh-Bonger, who describes their meeting in the Introduction to the *Complete Letters:* 'How thankful we were when it was at last time for Theo to go to the station! From the Cité Pigalle [where Theo was living at the time] to the Gare de Lyon was a long distance; it seemed an eternity before they came back. I was beginning to be afraid that something had happened when at last I saw an open fiacre enter the Cité; two merry faces nodded to me, two hands waved—a moment later Vincent stood before me. I had expected a sick man, but here was a sturdy, broad-shouldered man, with a healthy color, a smile on his face, and a very resolute appearance... Then Theo drew him into the room where our little boy's cradle was; he had been named after Vincent. Silently the two brothers looked at the quietly sleeping baby—both had tears in their eyes.'

Auvers-sur-Oise, an artists' village north of Paris, is the home of several painters, including Daubigny and Cézanne, and of a group of etchers, all of whom work with Dr Paul Gachet, who was an artist himself. Dr Gachet takes Vincent under his care. 'I have seen Dr Gachet, who gives me the impression of being rather eccentric, but his experience as a doctor must keep him balanced enough... He piloted me to an inn where they ask 6 francs a day. All by myself I found one where I shall pay 3.50 fr. a day.' (L.635)

'I often think of you, Jo, and the little one, and I notice that the children here in the healthy open air look well... I am working at his [Dr Gachet's]

Farmhouse in Auvers with Two Figures / Auvers-sur-Oise, July 1890   oil / canvas, 38 × 45 cm

Portrait of Dr Gachet. Sketch in letter 638/Auvers-sur-Oise, 3 June 1890

portrait, the head with a white cap, very fair, very light, the hands also a light flesh tint, a blue frock coat and a cobalt blue background, leaning on a red table, on which are a yellow book and a foxglove plant with purple flowers.' (L.638)

The same day he writes to his sister Wil: 'It was a great happiness to me to see Theo again, and to make the acquaintance of Jo and the little one... As for myself, the traveling and all the rest have come off very well so far, and coming back north has been a great distraction for me. And then I have found a true friend in Dr Gachet, something like another brother, so much do we resemble each other physically and also mentally... Every week I shall go stay at his house one or two days in order to work in his garden, where I have already painted two studies, one with southern plants, aloes, cypresses, marigolds; the other with white roses, some vines and a figure, and a cluster of ranunculuses besides... I brought along a relatively large picture for Theo's and Jo's little boy—which they hung over the piano—white almond blossoms—big branches against a sky-blue background—and they also have a new portrait of the Arlésienne in their apartment... The portrait of the Arlésienne has a drab and lusterless flesh color, the eyes calm and very simple, a black dress, the background pink, and with her elbow she is leaning on a green table with green books.' (L.W22)

While he was in Paris Vincent had seen a beautiful painting by Puvis de Chavannes at the Salon de Champ-de-Mars. It made a deep impression on him, and he continues in his letter to his sister: 'There is a superb picture by Puvis de Chavannes at the exhibition. The figures of the persons are dressed in bright colors, and one cannot tell whether they are costumes of today or on the other hand clothes of antiquity. On one side two women, dressed in simple long robes, are talking together, and on the other side men with the air of artists;

Old Vineyard with Peasant Woman/Auvers, end May 1890   pencil, brush, washed with blue, red and white gouache, 43.5 × 54 cm

in the middle of the picture a woman with her child on her arm is picking a flower off an apple tree in bloom. One figure is forget-me-not blue, another bright citron yellow, another of a delicate pink color, another white, another violet. Underneath their feet a meadow dotted with little white and yellow flowers. A blue distance with a white town and a river. All humanity, all nature simplified, but as they *might* be if they are not like that... a strange and happy meeting of very distant antiquities and crude modernity.' (L.W22)

In an unfinished letter to Gauguin, Vincent gives his impressions of Paris, and describes the last picture he had painted in Provence. 'Thank you for having written to me again, old fellow, and rest assured that since my return I have thought of you every day. I stayed in Paris only three days, and the noise, etc., of Paris had such a bad effect on me that I thought it wise for my head's sake to fly to the country; but for that I should soon have dropped in on you... I still have a cypress with a star from down there, a last attempt—a night sky with a moon without radiance, the slender crescent barely emerging from the opaque shadow cast by the earth—one star with an exaggerated brilliance, if you like, a soft brilliance of pink and green in the ultramarine sky, across which some clouds are hurrying. Below, a road bordered with tall yellow canes, behind these the blue *Basses Alpes,* an old inn with yellow lighted windows, and a very tall cypress, very straight, very somber. On the road, a yellow cart with a white horse in harness, and two late wayfarers. Very romantic, if you like, but also *Provence,* I think.' (L.643)

There is nothing in the letters which Vincent wrote in the last two months of his life to suggest that

Cypresses/Saint-Rémy, February 1890   oil/canvas, 43.5 × 27 cm

he was contemplating suicide. Their tone is sometimes melancholy, but he orders fresh paints from Theo and tells him he is excited by the idea of painting from models again. He also draws inspiration from the summer landscape: 'Here are three sketches—one of a peasant woman, big yellow hat with a knot of sky-blue ribbons, very red face, rich blue blouse with orange spots, background of ears of wheat... Then the horizontal landscape with fields, like one of Michel's, but then the color is soft green, yellow and green-blue. Then the undergrowth around poplars, violet trunks running across the landscape, perpendicular like columns; the depths of the wood are blue and at the bottom of the big trunks, the grassy ground full of flowers, white, pink, yellow and green, long grass turning russet, and flowers.' (L.646)

And even in the last letter he sends to Theo it is the voice of the inspired artist that speaks: 'Perhaps you will look at this sketch of Daubigny's garden. It is one of my most purposeful canvases. I add a sketch of some old thatched roofs and the sketches of two size 30 canvases representing vast fields of wheat after the rain... Daubigny's garden, foreground of grass in green and pink. To the left a green and lilac bush and the stem of a plant with whitish leaves. In the middle a border of roses, to the right a wicket, a wall, and above the wall a hazel tree with violet foliage. Then a lilac hedge, a row of rounded yellow lime trees, the house itself in the background, pink, with a roof of bluish tiles. A bench and three chairs, a figure in black with a yellow hat and in the foreground a black cat. Sky pale green.' (L.651)

On 27 July 1890 Vincent attempts to shoot himself, probably in fear of a renewed crisis. He had been out all day, and in the evening he returns to the inn where he is staying. The innkeeper sends for Dr Gachet, who notifies Theo in Paris. Theo stays by his brother's bedside until 29 July, when

The Garden of Daubigny. Sketch in letter 651/Auvers-sur-Oise, 24 July 1890

Vincent dies, calm and resigned.
Before the funeral Vincent's friends come from Paris and decorate his room with flowers and his own paintings. Vincent van Gogh is buried in the churchyard at Auvers-sur-Oise, in the midst of the wheatfields.
Theo, who only survived his brother by six months, lies buried beside him.

Sketches of Auvers-sur-Oise in letter 646/Auvers-sur-Oise, 1 July 1890

The Château d'Auvers/Auvers-sur-Oise, June 1890   oil/canvas, 50 × 101 cm

Crows in the Wheatfields/Auvers-sur-Oise, June/July 1890   oil/canvas, 50.5 × 103 cm

1853

Vincent is born on 30 March at Zundert (North Brabant), the eldest son of Theodorus van Gogh, Protestant clergyman, and Anna Carbentus.

1857

Theo, his brother, is born on 1 May.

1864

Until the summer of 1866 Vincent attends a boarding school in Zevenbergen, and

1866

then goes to a secondary school in Tilburg until March 1868.

1869

At the age of 16 Vincent becomes a junior clerk at Goupil & Cie. in The Hague, a branch of the Paris art dealers, where his Uncle 'Cent' is a partner.

1873

From June 1873 to October 1874 he works at the London branch of Goupil's.

1874–1876

In October he is transferred to Goupil's in Paris for a few months. In 1875 he returns briefly to London, and in May is transferred permanently to Paris. However, he is becoming increasingly disenchanted with the art trade, and on 1 April 1876 he is dismissed from the firm. His thoughts turn to religion. From April to July 1876 he works as an assistant teacher at a school run by Mr Stokes in Ramsgate, England, and then at Mr Jones's school in Isleworth, where he also preaches.

In December he returns to the Netherlands and his family, who have moved to Etten, North Brabant.

1877

From January to the end of April he works in a bookshop in Dordrecht. In May he moves to Amsterdam to prepare himself for the study of theology at the university.

1878

After a year he abandons his studies and spends three months at a college for evangelists in Brussels, on Mr Jones's advice. In November he is sent to Wasmes, a village in the Borinage, the southern mining region of Belgium, where he preaches and identifies with the plight of the poor.

1879

In July he is dismissed by the Brussels Evangelists' Committee for excessive zeal. He remains in the region for another year as an evangelist, living in Cuesmes, and gradually realizes that he wants to devote his life to art. He begins to draw.

1880

In October he leaves for Brussels, where he stays for six months. He studies anatomy and takes lessons in perspective drawing. He is befriended by Anthon van Rappard (1858–1892), a fellow-student. Meanwhile, Theo van Gogh is working for Goupil & Cie. in Paris, and begins sending Vincent a small monthly allowance.

1881

From April till October Vincent lives with his parents at the vicarage in Etten. He falls in love with his cousin Kee Vos, but is rejected, and after an argument with his parents he leaves for The Hague. There he is given lessons in drawing and painting by Anton Mauve, his cousin by marriage. He begins collecting French and English woodcuts from illustrated magazines, and meets several artists of the Hague School.

1882

He lives with the prostitute Sien Hoornik and her children, to the distress of his friends and family.

1883

In September he breaks all contact with The Hague and goes to Drenthe. He stays in Nieuw Amsterdam until December. Loneliness drives him back to his parents, who have moved to Nuenen.

1884

He paints the peasant life of Brabant. In January his mother breaks her leg, and Vincent's devoted nursing brings about a reconciliation with his parents.

1885

His father dies suddenly in March, and Vincent moves into a studio which he rents from the sexton of the Roman Catholic church in the village. At the end of November he leaves for Antwerp, where he studies Rubens and starts collecting Japanese prints, with which he decorates the walls of his room.

1886

He enrolls in the academy at Antwerp, but has serious disagreements with his teacher in the short time he is there. At the beginning of March he arrives unannounced in Paris. He is ill, and moves in to live with Theo. For a while he works in the studio class of the painter Fernand Cormon, where he meets Toulouse-Lautrec and Bernard. In June he and Theo move to a larger apartment in Montmartre, where he has his own studio. He meets impressionist painters.

1887

At the beginning of the year he organizes an exhibition of Japanese prints, followed by a show of his own work and that of his friends. Vincent, Bernard and Signac go on painting expeditions on the outskirts of Paris and along the Seine.

1888

On 20 February he leaves for Arles to escape the pressures of city life. He rents the 'yellow house', and paints in Arles and in nearby towns like Saintes-Maries-de-la-Mer on the Mediterranean. From 20 October to 24 December he shares his house with Gauguin, with financial assistance from Theo. The collaboration is fruitful but ends in a violent quarrel. Overwrought, Vincent cuts off part of his ear, and is taken to hospital.

1889

Vincent returns to the 'yellow house' at the beginning of the year and starts painting again. He has another crisis, and is readmitted to hospital. In May he voluntarily enters the Asyl St-Paul-de-Mausole in Saint-Rémy.

1890

He travels to Paris by train in May. He stays with Theo, his wife and their child for three days, and then goes on to Auvers-sur-Oise, where Dr Gachet, a painter, art-lover and friend of the impressionists, will keep an eye on him. On 29 July Vincent dies two days after shooting himself.

1891

Theo dies on 21 January.
Since 1914 the two brothers have lain side by side in the churchyard at Auvers-sur-Oise.

Address

National Museum Vincent van Gogh
Paulus Potterstraat 7
1071 CX Amsterdam
Tel. 020 - 76 48 81

How to get there
From Amsterdam Central Station:
tram no. 16 to Concertgebouw stop
tram no. 2 to Van Baerlestraat stop
From Amsterdam Zuid Station:
tram no. 5 to Van Baerlestraat stop

Opening hours
Tuesday to Saturday from 10 a.m. to 5 p.m.
Sundays and public holidays from 1 p.m. to 5 p.m.
Closed on Mondays and New Year's Day

Collections
Paintings and drawings by Vincent van Gogh
and his contemporaries, letters by and about
Vincent van Gogh, Japanese woodcuts,
engravings, archive

Library

Visual arts workshop

Reproduction department
Postcards, slides, reproductions, catalogues,
books

Restaurant and terrace
In the museum

Admission
There is an admission charge

Cloakroom
For walking sticks, umbrellas and bags

Exhibitions
From the permanent collection,
and temporary exhibitions

Colophon
Author: Lili Jampoller
Translation: Michael Hoyle
Advisers: Management and staff
                          of BV 't Lanthuys
                          and Rijksmuseum
                          Vincent van Gogh
Photographs: Thijs Quispel,
                          Gerda van der Veen,
                          Jan and Fridtjof Versnel
Typography: Dick Elffers
Illustrations copyright: BV 't Lanthuys
Printed by: steendrukkerij
                          de Jong & Co. – Hilversum
First published: March 1986

Excerpts from: The Complete Letters of Vincent
Van Gogh. Reprinted by permission of Little, Brown
and Company in association with New York
Graphic Society Books.